Matter and Materials

John Clark

Consulting Editor: Richard Hantula

GARETH**STEVENS**
PUBLISHING
A Member of the WRC Media Family of Companies

Please visit our web site at: **www.garethstevens.com**
For a free color catalog describing Gareth Stevens Publishing's
list of high-quality books and multimedia programs,
call 1-800-542-2595 (USA) or 1-800-387-3178 (Canada).
Gareth Stevens Publishing's fax: (414) 332-3567.

Library of Congress Cataloging-in-Publication Data

Clark, John.
  Matter and materials / John Clark. — North American ed.
    p. cm. — (Real world science)
  Includes index.
  ISBN 0-8368-6307-0 (lib. bdg.)
  1. Matter—Properties—Experiments—Juvenile literature. I. Title. II. Series.
  QC173.36.C56   2006
  530—dc22   2005054148

This North American edition first published in 2006 by
Gareth Stevens Publishing
A Member of the WRC Media Family of Companies
330 West Olive Street, Suite 100
Milwaukee, WI 53212 USA

This U.S. edition copyright © 2006 by Gareth Stevens, Inc. Original edition
copyright © 2001 by Haldane Mason Ltd. First published in 2001 by Red Kite Books,
an imprint of Haldane Mason Ltd., PO Box 34196, London NW10 3YB, U.K.
Email: info@haldanemason.com. Website: www.haldanemason.com

Editor: Ambreen Husain
Inside design: Rachel Clark
Illustrators: Phil Ford and Peter Bull Studios
Educational Consultant: John Stringer BSc
Gareth Stevens editor: Leifa Butrick
Gareth Stevens art direction: Tammy West
Gareth Stevens cover design: Dave Kowalski
Gareth Stevens production: Jessica Morris & Robert Kraus

Picture credits: © Corel: cover; Balfour Beatty 20; Bruce Coleman Collections/Mark Taylor 7, Jeff Foott 13b,
/Johnny Johnson 10, /Dr. Eckart Pott 25, /Kim Taylor 26; Eye Ubiquitous/Bennett Dean 18; Sidney Francis
14; Image Bank 4; Oxford Scientific Films/London Scientific Films 9, /Colin Monteath/Hedgehog House
13t, /David Cayless 21, 23, /Robert Winslow 29; Re-Cycle 30; Science Photo Library/Oscar Burriel 17.

Printed in the United States of America

1 2 3 4 5 6 7 8 9 10 09 08 07 06

Contents

The Material World

Everything around you that you can see or touch is made of matter. So are some of the things you can't see, such as the air. In fact, all the objects in the universe, from an exploding star to the hairs on your head, are made of matter. So "matter" is really just another word for "stuff." There are three main kinds of matter: solids, such as rock; liquids, such as water; and gases, such as air. This book is all about matter and the interesting ways it behaves.

Make the most of matter

There is an amazing array of materials – different kinds of matter – around us. Some are natural, such as wood and cotton, and some are artificial, such as plastic and fiberglass. Others are a combination of two or more materials. To help understand all these different materials, scientists sort them into groups depending on their physical and chemical properties. What does that mean?

Physical properties of a material include things like strength, heaviness, and flexibility. For example, can the material be stretched or bent, or does it break? Does it conduct (carry) electricity or heat well? How much weight can it hold? How heavy is it for its size? How hot does it have to be before it melts?

Chemical properties have to do with what happens to materials when they are burned or mixed together. For example, does a material catch fire easily? Does it dissolve in water? Does it mix with other materials? Is it safe to eat, or is it a poison?

So what's the point of all this? Well, knowing a material's physical and chemical properties helps us understand how to make the best use of it. That's why bridges are made of steel instead of tape, and why we use dish-washing liquid instead of wallpaper paste to clean our dishes. The more we know about materials, the easier it is to come up with new inventions to improve our lives.

Kites are made from paper or plastic because those materials are light and flexible.

TRY THIS

Sort it out

Collect various things made from different materials – a stone, a paper clip, a stainless steel teaspoon, a coin, a plastic bag, a piece of cooking foil, an eraser, or whatever else you can find. Now arrange them in various groups. For example, put all the things that are hard in one group, and all the things that are soft in another. Or divide them up into a group of things that are easy to squash when you squeeze them and a group of things that aren't. You could also split them up according to whether they seem heavy for their size or light. Use a magnet to test which things are magnetic and which are not. How many other ways of sorting them can you think of?

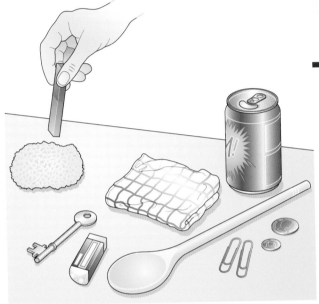

Amazing Fact

The bones inside your body are stronger for their size and weight than steel – and so is a single hair from your head.

Did You Know?

Plastics account for up to one-third of the materials that make up a modern car. They are also used to make TV sets, sneakers, computers, clothing, bowls, bags . The list seems endless. Plastics are fantastic because they can easily be molded into the shapes we want. The first plastic-like materials came from nature. They included rubber, made from the sap of a tropical tree, and cellulose, the main substance in plant fibers. Today, most plastics come from the chemistry lab. There are now dozens of plastics, and their names often begin with "poly–," such as polyethylene. Can you think of any more?

You use many different plastics every day.

Rock Solid

When we want to describe how firm and strong something is, we often say it's "as solid as a rock." Other solid materials include bricks, concrete, wood, most metals, and most plastics. All solids have some things in common. If they are small enough, we can take hold of them and pick them up. They are usually rigid and keep their shape. What is it about solids that makes them like this?

Inside a solid

Everything – solid, liquid, or gas – is made up of tiny particles called atoms. They are so tiny that you can see them only through a very powerful microscope. It would take several million of them side by side to match the thickness of the paper you are looking at. Atoms can join together in combinations called molecules.

The atoms or molecules inside a solid are packed closely together. They can hardly move from their positions, and that is why a solid keeps its shape. In many solids, the atoms or molecules always have the same regular arrangement. These solids are called crystals (see pages 18 – 19 for more crystal facts).

Mighty metals

Metals are one of the most important kinds of solid. They are strong and can be formed into different shapes. If you leave a metal spoon standing in a hot drink, the spoon handle soon gets hot as well. This is because metals are good conductors (carriers) of heat. That's why metals are used to make saucepans. The wires that carry electricity around your house are made of copper, another metal, because metals are also good conductors of electricity.

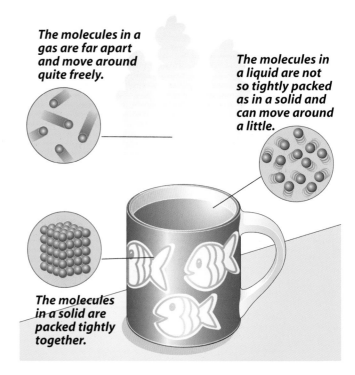

The molecules in a gas are far apart and move around quite freely.

The molecules in a liquid are not so tightly packed as in a solid and can move around a little.

The molecules in a solid are packed tightly together.

Rubber is elastic because of the shape of its molecules, which take the form of long zig-zag chains. When you stretch rubber, you pull the chains straight. But when you let go, the molecules snap back to their original shape.

Current conductors

You can test whether a material is a conductor of electricity by including it in a simple circuit using a battery and a lightbulb in a bulb holder. You'll also need three lengths of insulated wire, four alligator clips, and tape. Tape the bare end of one wire to one end of the battery, and attach a clip to the wire's other end. Clip it to the bulb holder. Tape the second wire to the other end of the battery and put a clip on its free end. Put clips on both ends of the third wire and clip one end of it to the bulb holder. Make sure the circuit works by touching the clips together. The bulb will light up. Now try completing the circuit with various materials, such as metals, carbon (sharpen a soft pencil at both ends to test the "lead"), and nonmetals. If the material conducts electricity, it will complete the circuit, and the bulb will light.

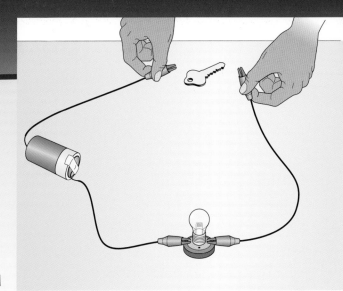

Did You Know?

You can disturb the regular arrangement of particles in a solid by heating it. Ice is a very common solid, especially in winter. In ice, water molecules are held in a regular structure. When you heat ice, the heat energy makes the molecules move about. As a result, the ice melts and becomes a liquid, which we know as water.

When ice or snow on branches or buildings slowly melts, the water produced may form icicles if the temperature falls below freezing.

Heat test

Get a metal spoon and a plastic spoon of the same size. Use a dab of butter to stick a frozen pea or a small candy near the end of each spoon handle. Put the spoons into a mug that is half full of hot water and watch what happens. The pea on the metal spoon slips off first because the metal spoon is better at conducting heat up its handle to melt the butter. Plastic, on the other hand, is a bad heat conductor.

Flowing Liquids

Unlike a solid, a liquid, such as water, has no fixed shape. It just takes up the shape of whatever you put it in because the atoms or molecules that make up a liquid are farther apart than in a solid. Although they are attracted somewhat to each other, they are free to move around more than in a solid. A liquid can splatter against a wall, break up into drops and join together again, and be poured, stirred, or spilled.

What's a liquid like?

Although the molecules in a liquid can move around, they resist being squeezed closer together. If you apply pressure at one place in a liquid, it is transmitted equally through the entire liquid. You can see this effect when you squeeze toothpaste out of a tube. Even if you squeeze at the very end of the tube, the paste still comes out at the other end. In the same way, a liquid can transmit a force. That's why liquids are used in hydraulic machinery, such as car brakes. The braking system is made up of tubes filled with liquid – brake fluid – and pistons that apply pressure to the liquid.

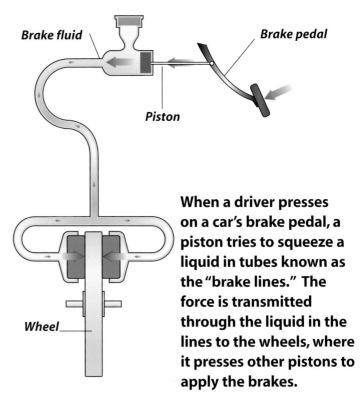

Brake fluid

Brake pedal

Piston

Wheel

When a driver presses on a car's brake pedal, a piston tries to squeeze a liquid in tubes known as the "brake lines." The force is transmitted through the liquid in the lines to the wheels, where it presses other pistons to apply the brakes.

Amazing Fact

Glass looks like a solid, but it's a liquid! It's a thick, or "viscous," liquid that moves very slowly, so slowly you can't see it move. Very old windows may have a wobbly surface from the glass flowing down the pane, while new windows have a flat surface.

Go with the flow

Liquids that are thick and sticky enough to be regarded as viscous include shampoo and honey. Oil is another important example. Its viscosity makes it a good lubricant because it tends to cling to the moving parts of machinery and reduce friction between the parts. A thinner liquid, such as water, would flow away.

The surface of a pool of water is like stretchy skin. That's why bugs like these water striders can walk across it without sinking.

On the surface

Have you ever watched insects walking on the surface of a pond? Water boatmen and water striders are two types of insects that can do this. Why don't they sink? The surface of the water seems to have a stretchy "skin," on which the insects walk. This "skin" is called surface tension, and it occurs because molecules of water cling together at the surface.

TRY THIS

Surface science

To see surface tension in action, you'll need a needle and a small square of tissue paper slightly larger than the needle. Fill a bowl nearly to the top with water. Place the needle on the tissue and carefully lay them on the surface of the water. The paper will soon soak through and sink, leaving the needle "floating" on the surface, held up by surface tension. What happens if you make a few waves with your fingers?

Did You Know?

Surface tension is what makes soap bubbles round. The tensions on the inside and outside surfaces of the thin film of liquid that forms the bubble pull it into the smallest shape possible, which is a ball, or sphere.

TRY THIS

Thick and thin

You can compare the viscosity (thickness) of liquids – as long as they're transparent. Try it with water, cooking oil, and a really thick syrup. (Be sure to ask whoever bought the syrup for permission to use it.) Take three jars or glasses and fill each of them with one of the liquids. Drop a marble into the water, and use a watch with a second hand to time how long it takes to fall to the bottom. Then do the same with the other liquids. Which takes the longest?

What a Gas!

Most gases are hard to find! You can't see them, smell them, or touch them, but they do exist. Air, which is made up of lots of gases, surrounds us all the time. There are also many other gases, such as the helium that fills fairground balloons and the natural gas we use for heating and cooking. Like a liquid, a gas has no fixed shape. Unlike a liquid, it will not stay in its container unless you put a tight lid on it.

Gas facts

The atoms or molecules that make up a gas are far apart. They zoom around constantly, bouncing off each other and off the walls of whatever container they happen to be in. As a result, the gas fills the container completely and pushes against its walls. This pressure can be put to good use. For example, the pressure of air inside car tires gives you a smooth ride. Compressed air also powers those jackhammers you see (and hear) being used to break up pavement.

The air we breathe is a mixture of gases. Only one-fifth of it is oxygen, which we need in order to live. About four-fifths of it is a gas called nitrogen. There are also traces of other gases, such as argon, neon, carbon dioxide, and water vapor (the gas form of water).

A lot of hot air

When air is heated, it expands. The warmer molecules move around more and spread out more. This makes the air lighter, so it begins to rise. Watching upside-down paper bags rise above a fire inspired the French brothers Joseph Michel Montgolfier (1740–1810) and Jacques Etienne Montgolfier (1745–1799) to experiment with hot-air balloons, leading in 1783 to the first human flight in a hot-air balloon.

On a large scale, air heated over warm ground rises in a column called a thermal. Glider pilots and soaring birds such as eagles use thermals to carry them upward. Thermals also play a big part in the weather. Warm air near the ground can hold a certain amount of water vapor. As it rises high in the sky, the air gets colder. The colder air can't hold as much water vapor, and some of the vapor condenses. It turns into droplets of water that form clouds. If the temperature gets even colder, the water droplets join together to form even larger droplets, and it rains.

Eagles use thermals to hover high above the ground while they scan the area below for prey.

English chemist Joseph Priestley (1733–1804) discovered oxygen in 1774. During his many experiments with gases, he dissolved carbon dioxide gas under pressure in water. The result was carbonated water. His discovery began a craze for soda water!

Soda pop and "sparkling" spring water have carbon dioxide in them. They are carbonated beverages. Next time you enjoy one, think of **Joseph Priestley!**

TRY THIS

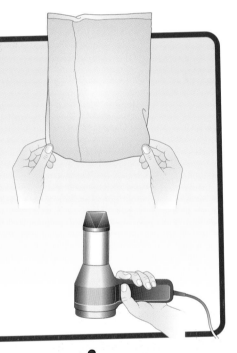

Hot-air balloon

An adult should help you with this. Take a large paper (not plastic) bag, about 8–10 inches (20–25 centimeters) square. Make sure there are no holes in it. Hold the bag with its mouth open and facing down. Now blow warm air from a hair dryer (on its low setting) into it. The warm air is less dense (and therefore lighter) than the cooler air outside the bag, so the bag will float upward when you let go of it. (Make sure you turn the hair dryer off first.) That is how a hot-air balloon works.

Did You Know?

Two important gases, hydrogen and helium, are less dense, and therefore lighter, than air. Because of their low density, both gases have been used for filling blimps and other airships. Hydrogen catches fire easily, however, which caused several disastrous airship crashes in the 1930s. Modern airships are usually filled with helium, which does not burn.

Amazing Fact

The gases argon, krypton, neon, and xenon occur in air in very small quantities and are sometimes called the rare gases. When electricity is passed through traces of these gases sealed inside a glass tube, the tube glows with color. Neon produces a bright red light. Neon lights are often used in store and street signs.

All Change

Whether a material is a solid, liquid, or gas depends on how its molecules move. This, in turn, depends on how hot or how cold it is. Heat a cold solid, and its molecules move farther apart until it melts. Heat the liquid, and its molecules move even farther apart until it forms a gas. These three forms – solid, liquid, and gas – are known as states of matter. Scientists call the change from one into another a "change of state."

State to state

The temperature at which a heated solid changes into a liquid is its melting point. The temperature at which a heated liquid changes into a gas or vapor is its boiling point. These changes of state are physical changes and can be reversed. Cool a gas enough, and it changes into a liquid. Keep on cooling the liquid, and it eventually turns back into a solid. The temperature at which a cooled liquid changes into a solid is its freezing point.

The change of a gas into a liquid when cooled is known as condensation. You can see condensation by breathing on a mirror. The water vapor in your breath condenses into tiny water droplets that form a misty film on the glass. A few solids, such as iodine and solid carbon dioxide (dry ice), are unusual because they can change directly from a solid into a gas. This is called sublimation.

When a candle burns, some of the wax melts in the heat of the flame. The hot liquid wax drips down the sides. As it cools, it becomes solid again.

Did You Know?

Deep below the ground, temperatures are much higher than at Earth's surface. This means that rock there may melt. When it gets even hotter, and pressure builds up, boiling hot, liquid rock is squeezed out of cracks in the surface, making a volcano. Once it reaches the air, molten rock – "lava" – soon cools and turns back into solid rock.

Amazing Fact

Mercury – the liquid in some thermometers and barometers – is a metal. Most metals melt into liquid only when they are incredibly hot. Mercury is the only metal that is liquid at normal room temperature.

A matter of size

Because a rise in temperature makes molecules move farther apart, most solids expand as they get hotter. Little spaces are built into bridges and railway lines to allow for expansion when it gets hot. Otherwise the structures would buckle as they increased in length. Also, most solids get smaller as they get cooler. Ice is different. It gets bigger when it cools. Ice in frozen water pipes can expand and burst the pipes if the temperature gets even colder. Ice is less dense, and thus lighter, than water – which is why icebergs and ice cubes float. Icebergs in the Antarctic can be larger than the tallest buildings and as long as 75 miles (100 kilometers), but they still float!

TRY THIS

Ice pressure

Get a plastic bottle (NOT a glass bottle), completely fill it with water, and screw the cap on tight. Place the bottle of water in a plastic bag and put it in the freezer. Leave it there for a day and then take it out. You'll probably find that the water expanded as it froze, bursting the bottle.

This iceberg is even larger than it looks because about 90 percent of an iceberg floats beneath the surface of the water.

Did You Know?

When water seeps underground and meets very hot rocks, it heats up and may rise to the surface to form a hot spring. If the undergound water becomes boiling hot, it may blast out of the surface as a column of steam and water called a geyser. Scientists are exploring how best to use this heat – called geothermal energy – as a source of clean power.

Yellowstone National Park in the western U.S. has many geysers. Some of them blast their columns of steam and boiling water at rather regular intervals.

13

Watery World

Water is a very important type of matter. Nearly three-fourths of Earth's surface is covered with it. Most of it is in the seas and oceans, but there is also water in lakes and rivers, as well as frozen water in the snow and ice around the Arctic and Antarctic ice caps. However, most water does not stay in one place. It moves around Earth in the water cycle.

The never-ending water cycle is vital for life on Earth.

Round and round

The energy that powers the water cycle comes from the Sun. The heat of the Sun warms the water in lakes, rivers, and oceans, which hold over 97 percent of the world's water. (Most of the remaining water is frozen in ice caps and in the large masses of ice called glaciers.) The heated water evaporates, changing into water vapor, which rises in the air. The vapor may form tiny water droplets that the wind moves around.

Higher in the atmosphere, water droplets gather together to form clouds. If the wind blows clouds off the sea and over land, or if clouds have to rise to get over mountains, they get cooler. This makes the vapor condense, and tiny droplets merge together to form larger drops. When these drops become too heavy to stay in the clouds, they fall as rain. If it's very cold, the raindrops may freeze and fall as hail, sleet, or snow.

Most of the rain falls in the oceans, where it starts the cycle over again, but some rain falls on the land. It flows into streams and rivers, which eventually flow back to the sea. In this way, water is constantly changing state, driven by the energy of the Sun.

Water vapor forms clouds

Water evaporates

Water vapor condenses, falling as rain, sleet, hail, or snow

Did You Know?

The ice in hail and snow is a type of solid crystal. Snow crystals have six-sided or six-pointed shapes, and every single one is different. Snowflakes form when the crystals join together as they fall, melt, and then freeze again. They reach the ground as snow only if the air temperature is freezing all the way down.

Snow crystals are made of frozen water vapor.

TRY THIS

Making clouds

Here's how to make a mini-cloud inside a bottle. Fill a plastic bottle with hot water from the tap. (Don't use boiling water.) Let it stand for a few minutes, and then pour out all but a quarter of the water. Now put an ice cube on the bottle's open top, and watch your cloud form! The ice at the top cools water vapor inside the bottle, so that the vapor condenses into tiny water droplets – just like a real cloud.

Amazing Fact

As hailstones tumble around inside a cold cloud, more and more ice crystallizes on them and they grow bigger and bigger – even as big as tennis balls with weights of up to 2 pounds (1 kilogram). They've been known to break windows and dent cars!

Did You Know?

Most of the ice in glaciers and the polar ice caps originally fell as snow. It was slowly squashed into ice under its own weight. Some parts of the Antarctic ice cap are more than 2 1/2 miles (4 km) thick. If the ice cap melted, world sea levels would rise by as much as 200 feet (60 meters).

15

Disappearing Act

A spoonful of sugar contains thousands of small crystals – as you'll notice if you spill them and have to clean up the mess. If you stir the hard sugar crystals in a glass of water, however, they disappear. At least they seem to. If you taste the water, you can tell the sugar is still there – so why can't you see it?

Simple solutions

Like most solid substances, sugar crystals are made up of millions of molecules. When you put them in water, the molecules can break free of each other. They are too small to see, but they are still there, floating around among the water molecules. This is called dissolving. The sugar has dissolved to form a solution. The thing that dissolves – in this case, sugar – is called the solute, and the liquid it dissolves in is called the solvent. Water is a solvent for many substances, which means there are lots of things that dissolve in water.

Not all substances are soluble (will dissolve) in water, and that's a good thing, too. How else could we drink water out of glasses, or sail boats in the water? Chalk, wax, and wood are all examples of substances that are insoluble (will not dissolve) in water. Can you think of others?

Many pills are made to dissolve in water. It makes them easier to take, and our bodies absorb them quicker in dissolved form.

There is a limit to how much sugar – or any other substance – you can dissolve in a given amount of water, but you can usually dissolve more of a substance if the water is hot. If you dissolve sugar in hot water, then let it cool, crystals will begin to appear again because cold water can't hold as much sugar as hot water can.

TRY THIS

Find the limit

Put some warm water in a jug or large jar and add spoonfuls of salt, stirring in between, until no more will dissolve. (Keep track of the number of spoonfuls you add.) You have made a "saturated" solution. Try the experiment again using the same amount of water at the same temperature, but dissolving sugar instead of salt. Which is the more soluble, salt or sugar? What happens if you use cold water?

Jelly is a type of gel. It comes in different colors and flavors.

Dissolving is just one of the ways one substance can be "dispersed" in (completely mixed in with) another. Here are some more:

▶▶ A gel (like the jelly you eat or hair gel) is a special combination of a liquid and a solid.
▶▶ Foam (like shaving foam or fire–extinguisher foam) is a gas dispersed in a liquid.
▶▶ An aerosol (like hair spray or spray paint) is a liquid dispersed in a gas.
▶▶ Smoke is a solid dispersed in a gas.

TRY THIS

Separating colors

A solvent can be used to separate mixtures. A simple way to see this is by using ink, which consists of a mixture of different pigments (colored substances). You will need a glass, some blotting paper, a black felt-tip pen, and tape. First, put about 1 1/2 inches (4 cm) of water in the glass. Next, cut a strip from the blotting paper about 1 1/2 inches wide and almost 1 inch (2 cm) shorter than the height of the glass. Make a big spot near one end using the felt-tip pen. Attach the other end of the strip to the middle of the pencil with tape. Balance the pencil on the top of the glass so that the strip dips into the water, but make sure

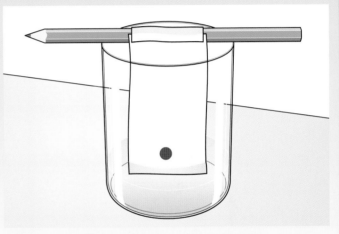

the spot is not in the water. As the water seeps up the paper, it will carry the pigments from the ink with it. Some move farther than others, and so the different pigments separate. Scientists often use this method, called chromatography, to separate mixtures. Try this with other colors and see what happens.

Amazing Fact

Almost 2 ounces (50 grams) of solid material leaves a person's body every day dissolved in urine. In some people some of this material may separate out of solution in a kidney and slowly form a large stone. Kidney stones sometimes weigh more than 2 pounds (1 kg).

Crystal Tips

A crystal has a regular structure of atoms or molecules. Most solids, apart from living things (and things that were once alive, like wood and cotton), are made up of crystals. Crystals have geometric shapes, but you can't always see the shapes because the crystals are too small. Some crystals have such beautiful shapes and colors that we wear them as jewelry.

Crystal clear

A perfect crystal has straight edges and flat, smooth "faces," or sides. Some crystals sparkle because their faces reflect the light when you move them around. Crystals that are valued for their beauty and rarity include gemstones such as diamonds, emeralds, and rubies.

The shape of a crystal depends on the arrangement of the atoms that make it up. For example, the atoms in salt are arranged in cube patterns, so salt crystals also take the shape of cubes. There are only six basic crystal shapes, and any one substance always has the same crystal shape. So all salt crystals, no matter where they come from, are cubes.

In hot countries with coastlines, such as India, people have salt farms. They collect the salt crystals that form when seawater in shallow pools evaporates under the heat of the sun.

To become a perfect crystal, a solid has to form freely with space around it, so that it doesn't get squashed. In nature, one of the main ways crystals form is that a molten substance cools and turns into a solid. Metals consist of crystals made in this way, and many kinds of rock contain crystals that grew as the molten rock slowly cooled and solidified. Some of these mineral crystals are as big as a car.

Crystals also form when a solution evaporates. For example, when a salt solution – salt dissolved in water – evaporates, the water turns into water vapor and floats away in the air, and the salt molecules join together into regular crystal shapes. This often happens at the edges of seas and salty lakes in hot countries.

Dish of crystals

Make a strong solution of salt by stirring several spoonfuls of it into a cup or jar of hot water. Put some of the salt solution in a saucer and leave it somewhere warm for a few days, such as on a window ledge in the sunshine. The water will evaporate away, and the dissolved salt will reappear as a deposit of crystals.

Amazing Fact

The numbers on digital watches and pocket calculators are made of patterns of liquid crystals held between two pieces of glass. Electricity is used to change the patterns of the crystals so that they form numbers. This is called an LCD, or liquid crystal display.

Did You Know?

Crystals can be used in jewelry, but they also have other uses. Diamond is the hardest substance in the world, so it is used to make drills for drilling down through rock to reach deposits of oil. Rotating disks used for cutting stone and concrete are also coated with industrial diamonds. Quartz crystals can be made to vibrate in a perfectly regular time sequence, so they are used in quartz clocks and watches. Silicon crystals are in the silicon chips that make computers work.

TRY THIS

Growing crystals

Make a strong sugar solution by adding as much sugar as will dissolve in a mug or jar of hot water. Next, take a short length of thick thread or thin string and tie one end to the middle of a pencil. Balance the pencil across the top of the jar so that the thread hangs into the solution. Then leave your experiment alone for a few days. After a while, sugar crystals will appear at the end of the thread. The longer you leave the thread hanging, the bigger the crystals will grow.

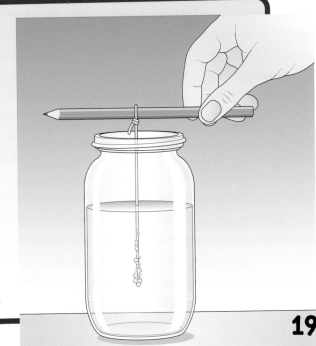

Mix and Match

Salt and water are easy to mix together. You just stir the salt in and it dissolves. Not all substances mix this easily. What about two solids, such as salt and sand? You can put them together, but neither one dissolves, and you can separate them again afterwards. Two liquids may mix perfectly, like vinegar and water, but other pairs of liquids can be very hard to mix.

In the mix

Solids, liquids, and gases can all be mixed together – some more easily than others – to make new materials. Cement can be made from clay, chalk, and water that is mixed together and put through a special process. This requires special equipment and takes a long time, but simply mix the cement with sand, gravel, and water, leave it for a while, and you have concrete – a very useful material!

You would think all liquids would mix – and many do, such as water and juice or tea and milk – but what happens if you try to mix oil and water? The oil just sits on top of the water. If you shake them together very hard (ideally in a bottle or jar with a lid), they will mix for a little while. If you leave the bottle to stand, the oil and water will gradually separate again.

Although oil and water don't like mixing, you can make them mix – and stay mixed – by mixing in a third substance called an emulsifier. A mixture with an emulsifier is called an emulsion – tiny blobs of a liquid dispersed in another liquid. Mayonnaise is an emulsion. Other common emulsions include cosmetics such as cold cream, which is made from an oil such as liquid paraffin or lanolin and combined with water, using soap as the emulsifier.

Concrete is used for the foundations of buildings and bridges, as well as in roads and pavements, because of its strength.

Amazing Fact

Some substances react so violently when they mix that they are used as rocket fuel. The thrusters that steer the space shuttle in orbit use fuel made from two chemicals that burst into flames as soon as they mix.

Clever coloring

Put equal volumes of cooking oil and water into a large glass jar. They will not mix but will form two layers, with the oil on top. Now carefully add a few drops of food coloring. It will sit as little drops, or globules, on the top, because it does not mix with oil. Use a spoon to stir the whole mixture. The food coloring will immediately mix with the water and color it. What happens to the oil?

Did You Know?

The same stuff used to wash dishes can help clear up an oil slick at sea! Detergents, such as dish liquid, break up grease so that water can wash it away. That's why they are used to wash clothes and dishes. They can also break up larger amounts of oil, such as oil spills at sea that can otherwise kill wildlife and damage beaches.

Separating solids

How do you separate salt and sand? One way requires a magnifying glass, a pair of tweezers, a steady hand, and lots of patience. It would take a long time. There's an easier way with a little help from science. Here's how it works. First make a sand-and-salt mixture by stirring together equal quantities of both in a jar of water until all the salt dissolves. Now pour the mixture through coffee filter paper or a strainer lined with a strong tissue. The sand stays on the paper, because sand doesn't dissolve in water. (If it did, beaches wouldn't last long!) Next, recover the salt from the water by letting the remaining solution evaporate. (Heating it helps.) The salt crystallizes out as the water evaporates.

All about Soil

Soil is one of the world's most important mixtures. It's a combination of water, gases, bits of rocks and minerals, and the remains of dead plants and animals. Nearly all plants, from small grasses to giant forest trees, need soil to grow in, and all animals ultimately depend on plants for food. So all of us owe our lives to soil.

In the mix

Soil is a mixture of different materials, but how do they get mixed together? Rainwater helps, and so do plant roots and burrowing animals such as worms. Still, soil has different layers. The dead plant and animal remains, called humus, are found in the uppermost layer of soil, while stones and fragments of rock are mostly found in the bottom layers. Soil in different parts of the world, or even within one garden, contains different mixtures of ingredients, which is why some plants thrive better in one place than in another.

In fact, scientists have identified thousands of different soil types! Sandy soils let water drain through them easily, while clay soils are sticky and heavy, so water doesn't drain through quickly. Loamy soils, much loved by gardeners, are a mixture of sand, clay, and silt; they are brown in color, drain well, and contain lots of humus. Chalky soil, on the other hand, is pale and stony, with little humus, and water drains through it very quickly.

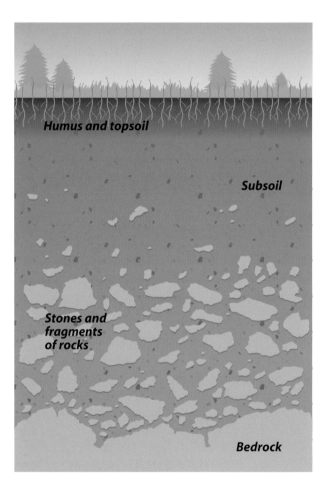

Humus and topsoil

Subsoil

Stones and fragments of rocks

Bedrock

Soil has different layers.

Soil science

Scientists study soil by separating it into its different parts. One way of doing this is to break up the soil as much as possible and then sift it into smaller and smaller particles. Another method is to stir a sample of the soil into water and then leave it to separate into layers. The biggest, heaviest bits fall to the bottom first, and the smallest bits end up on top.

Soil study

Collect two or three small samples of soil from different places, such as your family's garden, a flowerpot, and a park.

To find the soil type, wet a small sample and rub it in the palm of your hand to see if it is smooth (clay-rich soil), gritty (sand-rich soil), or spongy with a fair amount of dark-colored humus (loamy soil).

To test the drainage, put a sample of soil in a funnel. Hold the funnel over a jar and pour in some water. How quickly does the water pass through?

To check the particle sizes, shake each soil sample through a kitchen strainer. How much passes through the strainer and how much is left behind?

To check the composition, add each soil sample to a jar of water, screw on the lid, and shake well. Then let the samples settle. You will see the different layers form, with

the densest layer (sand and stones) at the bottom and the lightest (clay) on top. Humus will float on the surface of the water.

Did You Know?

Along with worms, spiders, and insects, soil is full of even smaller living beings. These creatures are not pests. They improve soil by digesting dead plants and animals and breaking them down into rich, fertile humus. Burrowing by soil creatures improves the texture of soil by letting air into it, but a few creatures harm plants by eating roots or spreading diseases.

Worms do a great job of mixing up soil and rotting plants in compost.

Chemical Reactions

If you dissolve salt in water, you can get it back by letting the water evaporate. If you mix sugar and sawdust, you can – if you're willing to spend a lot of time – pick out the sugar again. But what happens if you set fire to a mixture of sugar and sawdust? After the smoke and flames died down, there would be nothing you could do to get the sugar and the sawdust back. That's because they have been part of a chemical reaction.

When you mix together and bake the ingredients of a cake, the heat changes them into a new – and very tasty – substance!

Changed forever

In a chemical reaction, two or more substances combine to make something entirely different. It's usually impossible to reverse the process. Millions of chemical reactions are taking place every second around us and even inside us. All the processes that keep our bodies growing and moving are made possible by chemical reactions.

Other everyday chemical reactions take place in cooking, inside batteries in flashlights and toys, and in fireworks and explosives. None of these reactions can be undone. For example, you can't "uncook" a cake and change it back into eggs, butter, sugar, and flour.

Burning question

There are many different types of chemical reactions. One of the most common is oxidation – combining a substance with oxygen. One of the most common types of oxidation is burning. Burning something – like sugar, sawdust, gasoline, or rocket fuel – is called combustion. In this reaction, the substance, or fuel, reacts with oxygen in the air to give off energy, as well as other substances. For example, when a fuel such as gasoline, oil, or candle wax burns, it gives off heat and light energy, plus water and a gas called carbon dioxide. Because humans burn so much fuel, we now have a problem with too much carbon dioxide, which some scientists think builds up in the air and helps cause a gradual increase in the temperature of Earth's surface known as global warming.

A chemical reaction called photosynthesis happens inside plant leaves. The plant combines water from the soil and carbon dioxide from the air using energy from the Sun. All these react to produce food that keeps the plant alive and helps it to grow.

TRY THIS

Inflating fizz

You will need a small, plastic carbonated-beverage bottle, a funnel, some baking soda, some vinegar, and a balloon. Pour a little vinegar into the bottle. Use the funnel to pour a spoonful of the baking soda into the balloon. Then carefully stretch the neck of the balloon over the neck of the bottle and lift up the balloon so that the baking soda falls into the vinegar. The vinegar reacts with the baking soda to produce carbon dioxide gas, which then begins to inflate the balloon.

Did You Know?

In a chemical reaction, things that react together are called reactants. The things that are created are called products. Reactants and products can be completely different from each other. For example, when sodium – a soft, silvery metal – reacts with chlorine – a poisonous, choking green gas – they turn into pure white sodium chloride crystals – otherwise known as ordinary salt.

Amazing Fact

In midsummer, an acre (0.4 hectare) of corn – about one and a third football fields – produces enough oxygen by photosynthesis every day for 130 people to breathe.

25

Oxidation Options

Burning is one type of oxidation – a reaction between a substance and the oxygen in the air. Oxidation can happen quite slowly (think of a barbecue or a log fire that can burn for hours) or very fast, as in a big explosion that gives off lots of heat and light. It can also happen very slowly indeed. Rusting, for example, is also a type of oxidation.

Many different substances containing metals help create the spectacular colors of fireworks explosions.

Reaction force

The simplest oxidation reaction happens when hydrogen burns in oxygen. The only product (apart from heat and light energy) is water. That's why space rockets, which run on hydrogen, are shrouded in clouds of steam at liftoff. It is also why engineers are trying to make cars that run on hydrogen instead of gasoline. Hydrogen cars would produce no carbon dioxide or other pollution.

In a big explosion, oxidation happens even faster. The force of the explosion comes from huge amounts of hot gases produced in the reaction. The shock wave from the explosion causes the bang.

Rusting is an example of very slow oxidation. Iron and steel become rusty when the metal combines with oxygen in the air, making a new chemical called iron oxide – or rust. There is no heat or light, but several years of rusting can destroy a car just as completely as a fast, hot fire.

Did You Know?

Gunpowder is the oldest known explosive. It is believed to have been discovered by Chinese scientists in the tenth century or earlier. The Chinese are also credited with the invention of fireworks.

Candle magic

Put a short, thick candle in a large glass bowl – a large mixing bowl will do – and carefully pour about 1 inch (2–3 cm) of water into the bowl. Ask an adult to light the candle and cover it with a large glass jar. Watch what happens. As the candle burns, it uses up the oxygen in the air inside the jar. The water keeps new air from getting into the jar. When all the oxygen is used up, the candle goes out. Without oxygen, the combustion reaction cannot continue.

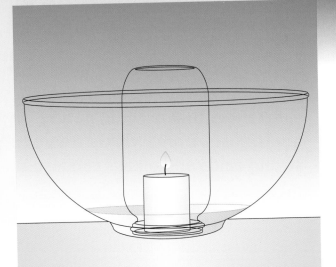

Burning is forever

Take a piece of paper and see what it feels like. Pull both ends of it to see how strong it is. Then, with the help of an adult, put the paper on the ground outside and burn it completely. What does it look like now? Can it be turned back into paper?

Amazing Fact

The planet Mars is known as the Red Planet because it is covered by soil that is red. And that's because the soil is rich in iron oxide – rust!

Did You Know?

When iron reacts with oxygen, it makes iron oxide – rust. There are forms of iron oxide that can be decorative rather than destructive. Pottery makers sometimes use a glaze containing iron on their pots. When the pots are baked in a kiln (oven) containing lots of oxygen, the iron is oxidized to a form of iron oxide that is red. If the kiln has only a little oxygen, the iron oxide formed is black.

Pottery makers can vary the oxygen level in their kilns to produce different shades of red and black.

Acid Test

Lemon juice and vinegar taste sour and sharp. They're acids. Baking soda tastes bitter and has a soapy feel. It's an alkali. Acids and alkalis are substances that occur in nature, and they are used in food and in all kinds of products, from wrinkle cream to toilet cleaner. Although they are useful, strong acids and alkalis can also be very dangerous.

Surrounded

Acids are all around us. Ants and stinging nettles have formic acid in their stings. Tartaric acid is found in grapes and other fruits, citric acid occurs in lemons and limes, and carbonic acid is present in soda water and other carbonated beverages.

Strong acids such as sulfuric acid (used in car batteries) are dangerous. They can burn your skin and clothing. There is a strong acid that occurs naturally in your stomach – hydrochloric acid – but it doesn't eat away your insides. It helps to digest food. You may feel it stinging your mouth if you have heartburn! Nitric acid is used to make fertilizers and explosives. All these acids are strong enough to dissolve metals.

Weak alkalis include baking soda and washing soda. They are used in baking powder and indigestion tablets. Strong alkalis such as sodium hydroxide (caustic soda) can cause nasty burns if they get on your skin. They are used in oven cleaners, for cleaning drains, and for making soap.

Bee stings contain many chemicals, including acids, which may cause the pain you feel if you're unlucky enough to get stung.

Neutralize

When an acid is mixed with an alkali, the two neutralize each other and react together to produce some type of salt and water. For example, hydrochloric acid reacts with sodium hydroxide to form sodium chloride, or common salt. A medicine containing an alkali is sometimes taken to ease the acid-caused pain of heartburn or acid indigestion.

Acid rain – rain with a weak acid in it – can kill trees and eat away at buildings and statues. A major cause of it is the burning of coal and oil at power stations. Gases from power stations react with water droplets in clouds to form such chemicals as sulfuric acid and nitric acid. These can be carried in clouds for many miles before falling to Earth as rain.

This statue has been damaged by acid rain.

TRY THIS

Make your own indicator

An indicator is a chemical that can change color to show if something is acid or alkali. With the help of an adult, chop up a red cabbage and boil it in some water. (If possible, use distilled water.) Throw away the cabbage, allow the purple liquid to cool, and filter it through a paper coffee filter or a strainer lined with a

tissue. Next, get several clean jars or glasses and put some of your cabbage juice indicator in each one. Now try dropping in them substances such as lemon juice, orange juice, baking soda, sour milk, vinegar, and laundry detergent. Acids will make the indicator turn red, while alkalis will make it turn greenish-blue.

Amazing Fact

Vinegar is a weak solution of a type of acid called acetic acid. It's used for making pickles (like pickled onions) because the acid kills the bacteria that would otherwise make the food go bad.

Trash or Treasure?

Every minute of every day, someone somewhere is using a material. All materials either occur naturally or are made by combining or changing natural materials. The paper used for the pages of this book was made from wood that came from trees. The plastic for plastic bags is made using oil that is found underground, but the world's supply of raw materials will not last for ever.

Think twice

Making a bridge, a car, or even a paper clip uses steel. Just think of all the aluminum used to make cans for soft drinks. Every time someone scraps a car or throws away a soft-drink can, the metal is gone forever, and more rubbish is produced. The same happens when a bottle or a magazine or anything else is thrown away.

Wood is the only raw material that can be replaced. New trees can be grown for making paper, but it takes many years for a tree to grow big enough to be used, so it makes sense to recycle or reuse as many materials as we can. Old newspapers and magazines can be used for making paper or cardboard. Empty glass bottles can be cleaned and used again, or crushed and melted to make new

Amazing Fact

The U.S. produces roughly 250 million tons of trash every year. Some experts think it could be used to produce as much energy as 100 million tons of coal, but most of it is buried in the ground instead.

ones. Plastics are more difficult to recycle because there are so many different kinds, and most don't rot, so plastic trash keeps increasing. Some plastics can be recycled, and now there are new plastics that will break up and rot away.

In this workshop, children are being taught how to repair and look after bicycles.

Did You Know?

Many old bicycles are thrown away or lie rusting in garages. Organizations like Bikes Not Bombs in the U.S. and Re-Cycle in Britain ship second-hand bicycles to developing countries. In poorer countries, many children walk miles to school and back every day. Most cannot afford a bicycle. With help from volunteers, children learn how to look after a bicycle. They can then ride off on a bike that might otherwise have ended up as trash!

Glossary

combustion
Burning; a chemical reaction in which a substance reacts with oxygen, yielding heat and light

condensation
The process in which a vapor or gas cools and changes into a liquid. When water vapor in the air cools, it condenses into tiny water droplet.

conductor
Something that lets electricity or heat pass through it

density
For a particular substance, the amount of mass, or matter, it has in a given amount of space

dissolve
To break down into tiny bits throughout a liquid when mixed with it

emulsifier
A substance used to blend together two liquids that will not otherwise mix

emulsion
Tiny bits of one liquid dispersed (fully mixed) in another liquid

evaporation
The process in which a liquid or solid warms and turns into a vapor or gas. As water heats up, it evaporates into water vapor in the air.

friction
A force between surfaces that are touching

indicator
A substance that shows whether a solution is an acid or an alkali by its color

insulator
Something that does not let electricity or heat pass through it or lets only a little pass through

lubricant
A substance, such as oil, that helps moving parts of a machine work together smoothly and with little friction

matter/material
What something is made of

molecule
A basic unit of a substance, consisting of atoms that are linked together

natural gas
Gas extracted from Earth that is used as a fuel and as a raw material for making various chemicals

oxidation
A chemical reaction between a substance and oxygen

photosynthesis
A chemical reaction by which plants use sunlight, water, and carbon dioxide to make food

piston
In automobile brake systems, a device used to help carry the braking force to the wheels. It is made up of a small cylinder that moves in and out in a slightly larger cylinder filled with liquid.

solidification
The process in which something turns into a solid, or solidifies

solute
A substance that dissolves in a liquid to form a solution

solution
A substance that is made when a solid is dissolved in a liquid

solvent
A substance in which a solid dissolves to form a solution

sublimation
The process in which a solid turns into a gas without becoming a liquid first

surface tension
An effect that makes a liquid seem to have a stretchy "skin." It is caused by the molecules of the liquid clinging together at the surface.

viscosity
How easily a substance flows. Water has a low viscosity and flows easily. Molasses is more "viscous" and flows more slowly

Index